Drowning

Drowning

Poetry & Art for a Pandemic-Weary World

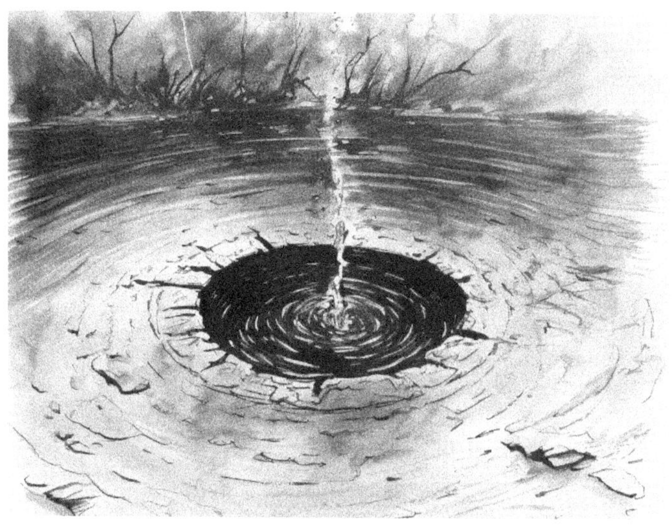

Tara Thiel

Balm in Gilead Press
Winston Salem,
North Carolina
27104

Published by Balm in Gilead Press
an imprint of Aphorisms Media, LLC.
The portrayal of a spilled medicine bottle is a trademark of
Aphorims Media, LLC.

FIRST EDITION

Book Design: Tara Thiel
Typeface: Arima Koshi
Art: Digital Collage of original works by Tara Thiel
and AI-generated works using Midjourney

Library of Congress Control Number: 2024900402

Paperback ISBN-13: 978-1-963491-00-5

Grateful acknowledgement is made to the editors of the following
publication, in which the poem listed first appeared: Global Warm-
ing; "The Neutrality of Drowning."

To Kris, Kaia, and Daniel

for always rescuing me
when I'm drowning

Contents

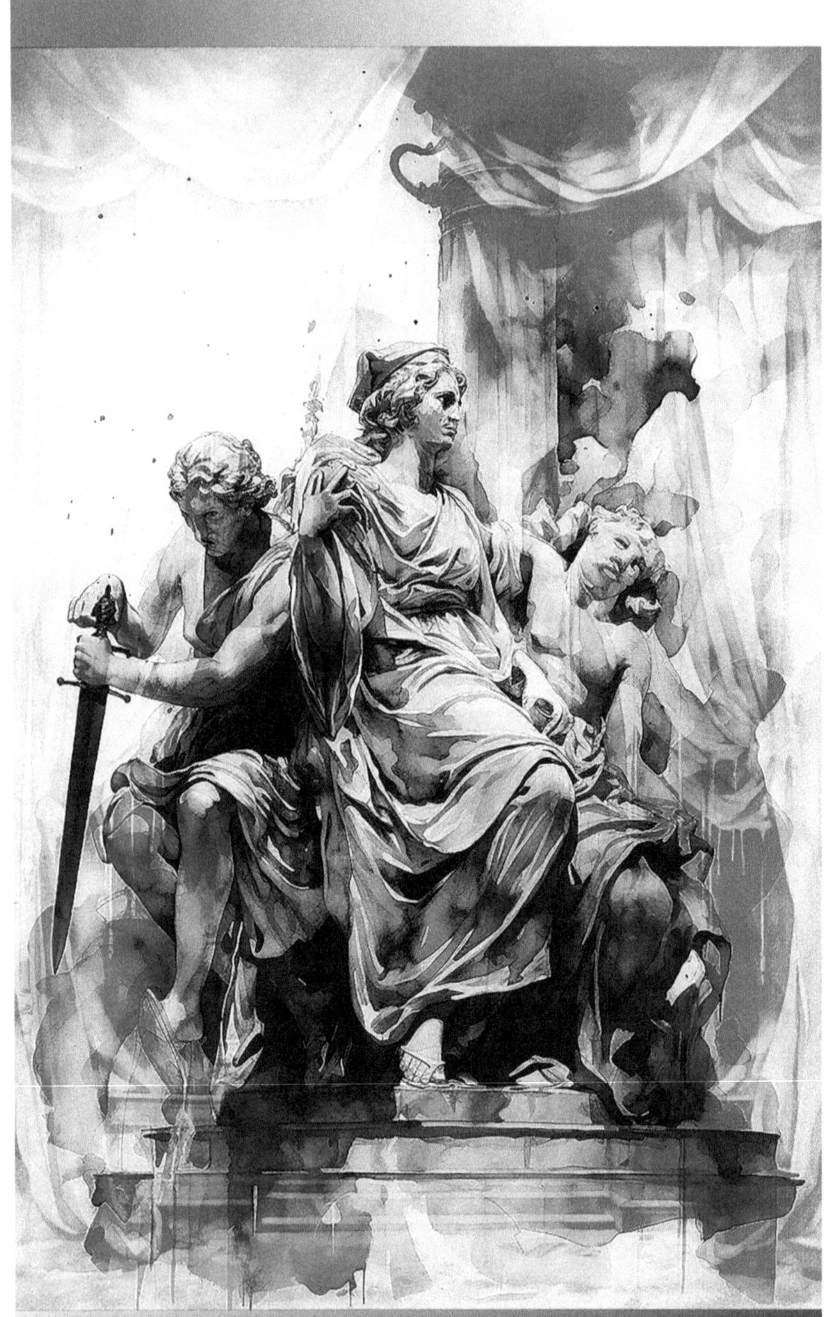

The Philosophy of Drowning

I drown in cultured pools
as a player entering stage left.
A murderer of horizons and purpose
flinging crudely fashioned weapons at the
divine heart. Morality buried beneath the floorboards
and driven into chaos by the furious pounding
and slow decomposition of a sunset-
colored sponge wrung out to dry.
I drown in cultured pools.

LEFT: The Song of Melancholy

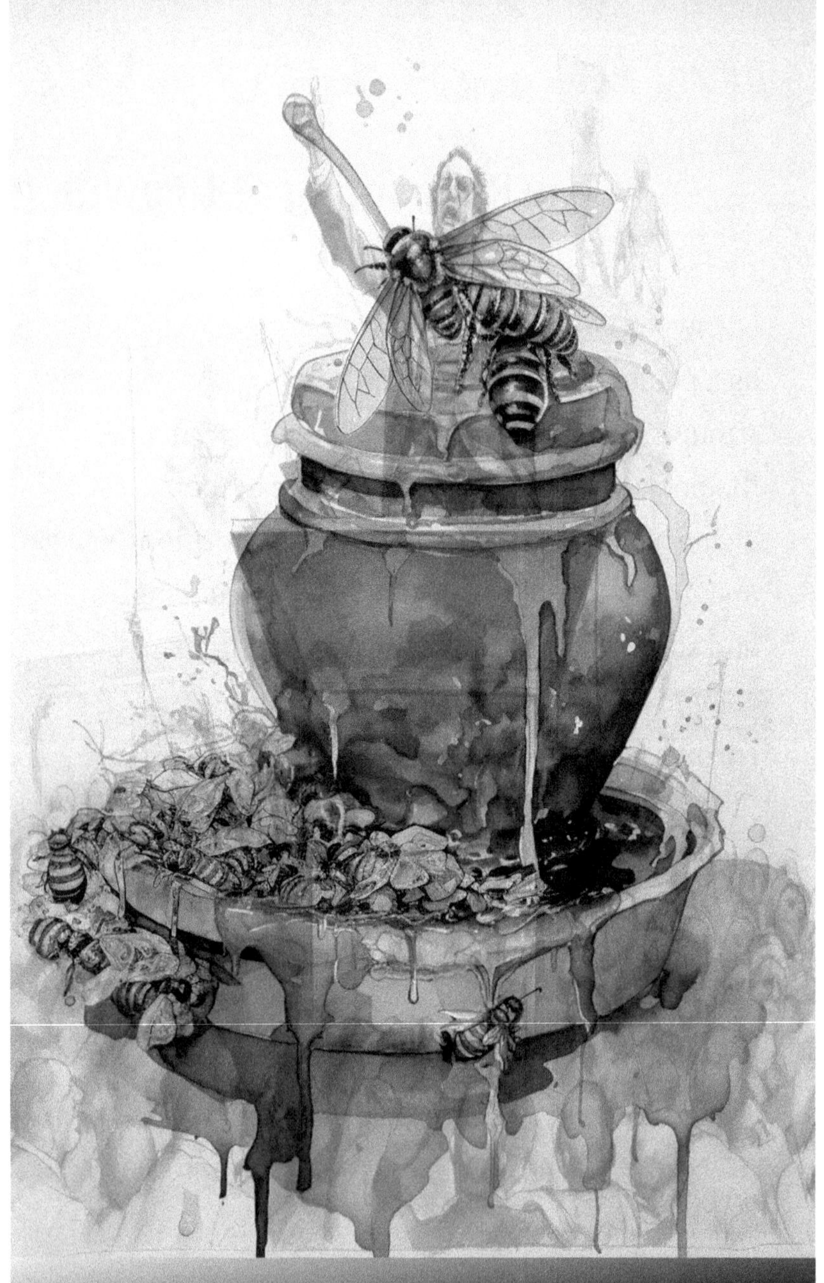

The Politics of Drowning

I drown in florid pools
of political rhetoric spilling
meaningless gabbed proclamations.
The bombastic grandiloquence of empty
thoughts, prayer and promises in soundbites.
Flamboyant speeches of colloquialisms
dripping honey from color-coded and
sugar-coated gums and tongues.
I drown in florid pools.

LEFT: The Song of Indulgence

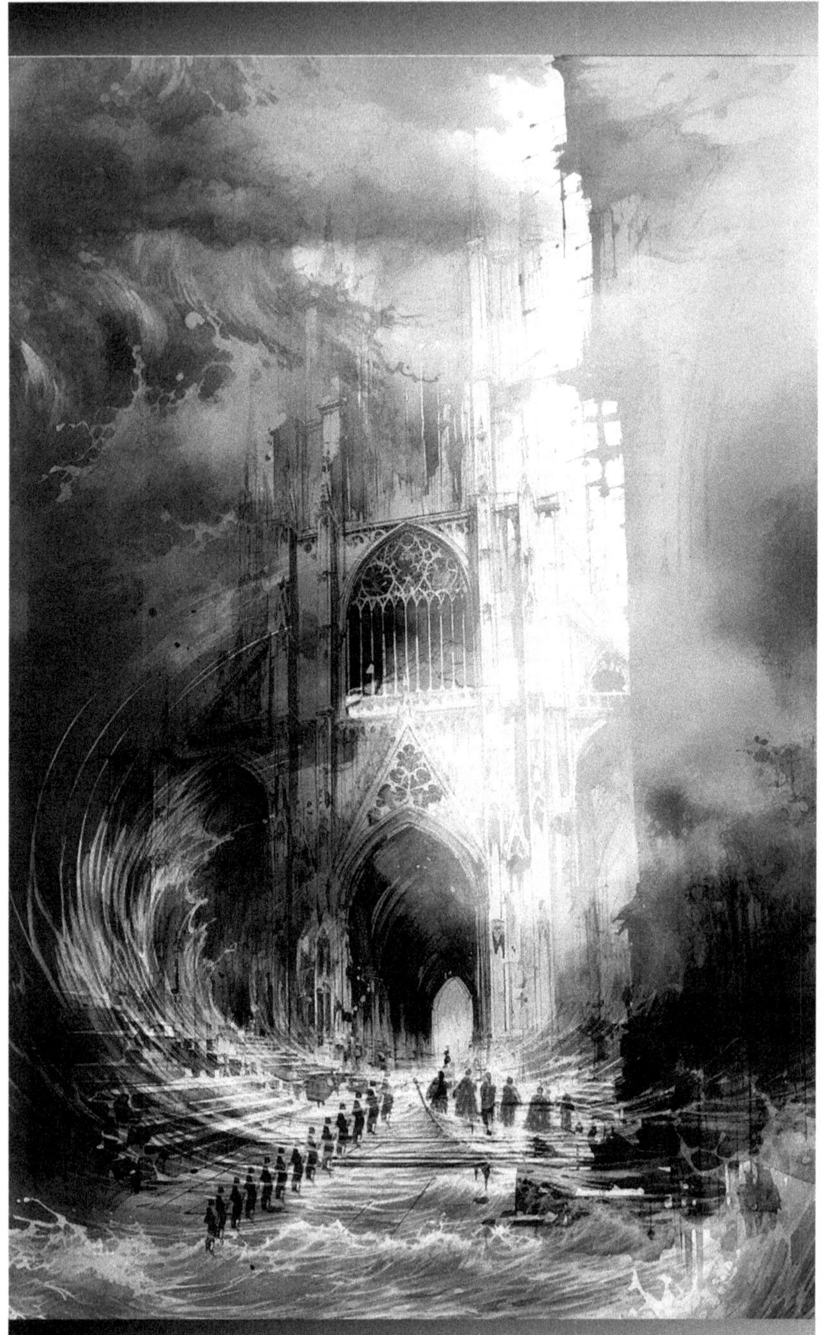

The Religion of Drowning

I drown in canonical pools

beneath the weight of original sin.

Mistaking divided waters for dry land's safety

until windswept in the depths, slamming against steel;

manmade walls of divine rebuke against the secular surge.

A promised peoples' rejection of equality in the escape

from purgatory, unable to see the ashen dust as

anything but sand: death on the beach.

I drown in canonical pools.

LEFT: The Song of Dissonance

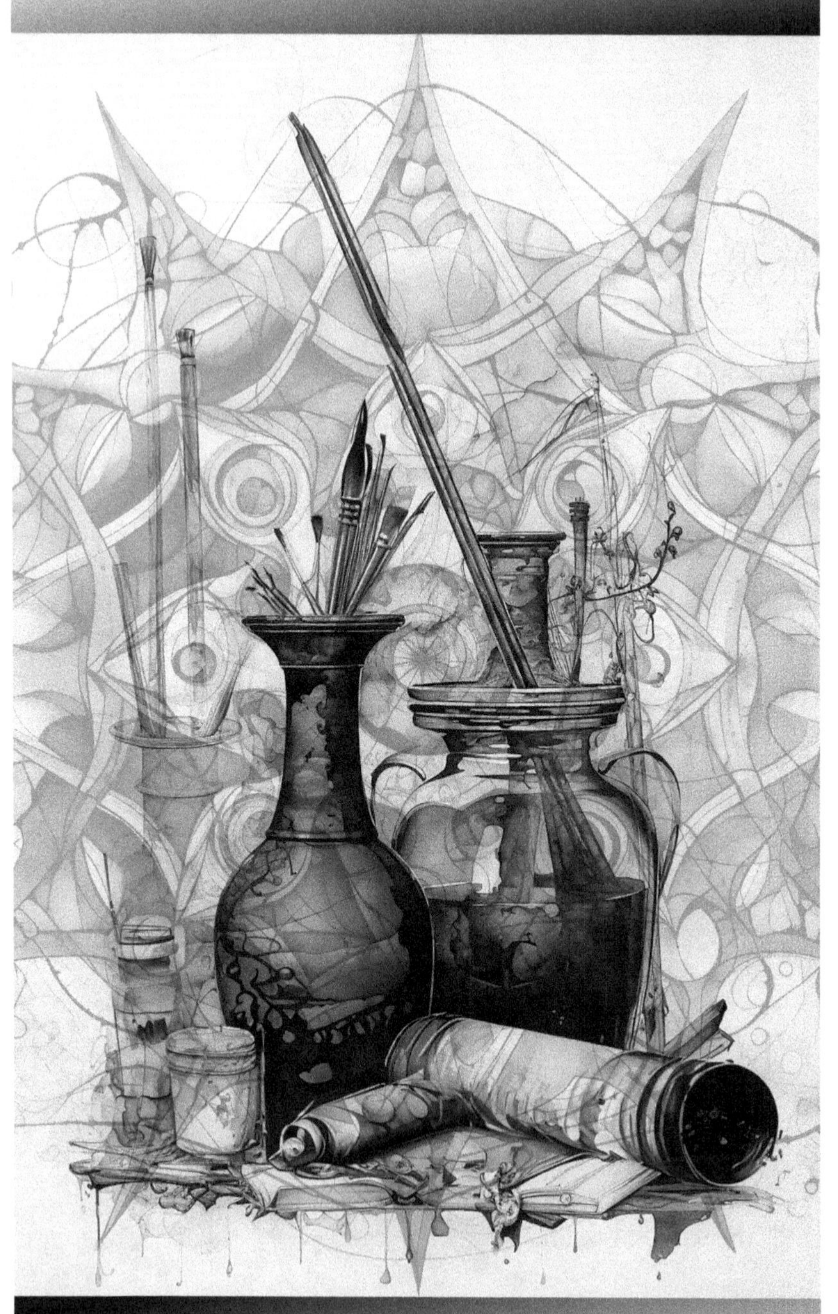

The Art of Drowning

I drown in lank pools
of salt and blood and paint
pounding wells into the canvas.
Prismatic waters and kaleidoscopic
ripples propagating unalterable streaks.
Deluge of mottled, macerated decay
of svelte paper overwhelmed by
apathy of the artless ruins.
I drown in lank pools.

LEFT: The Song of Ascetism

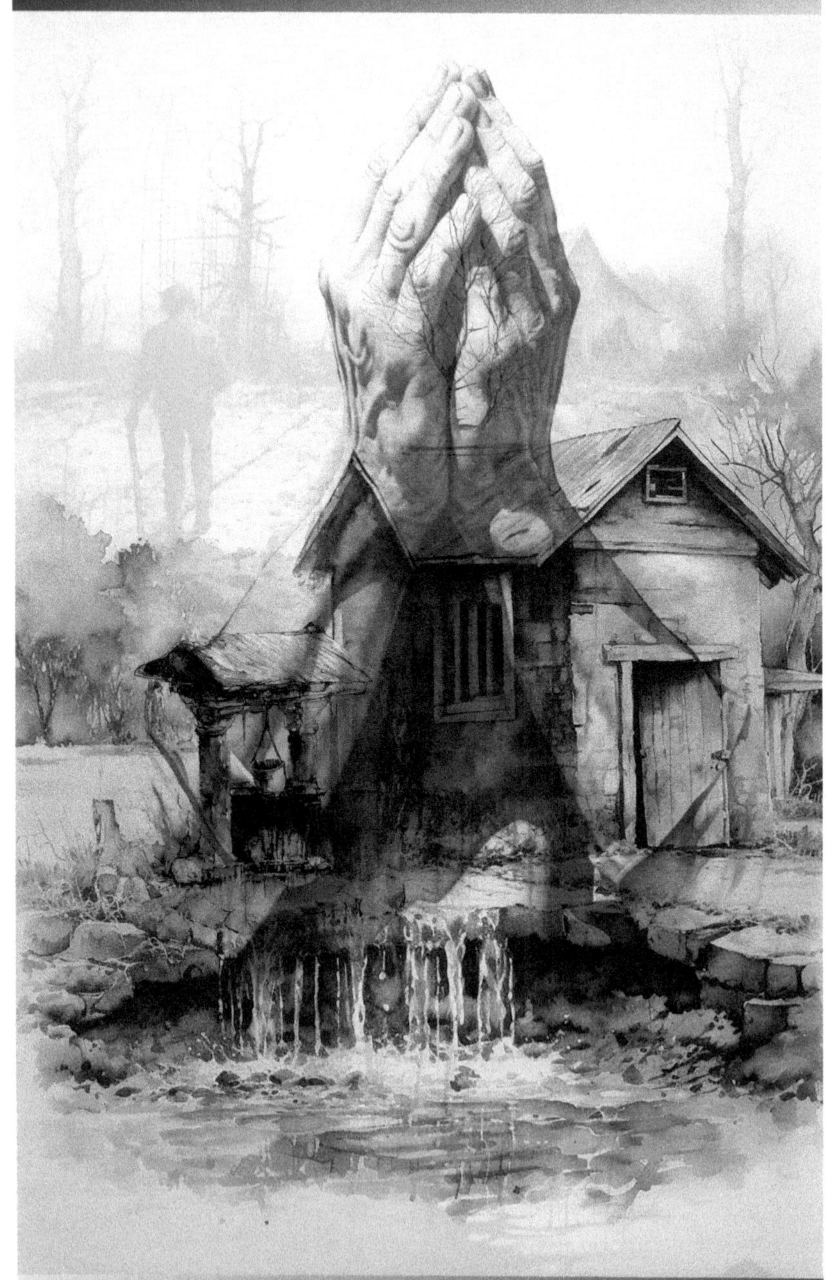

The Skill of Drowning

I drown in bound pools
of unworthiness emanating
copiously from gaping wounds.
Complicated waters of wretched
generations, unfulfilled and aggrieved.
Inhaling ancestral guilt, exhaling
erudite compunction, choking
on cultivated inadequacies.
I drown in bound pools.

LEFT: The Song of Flagellation

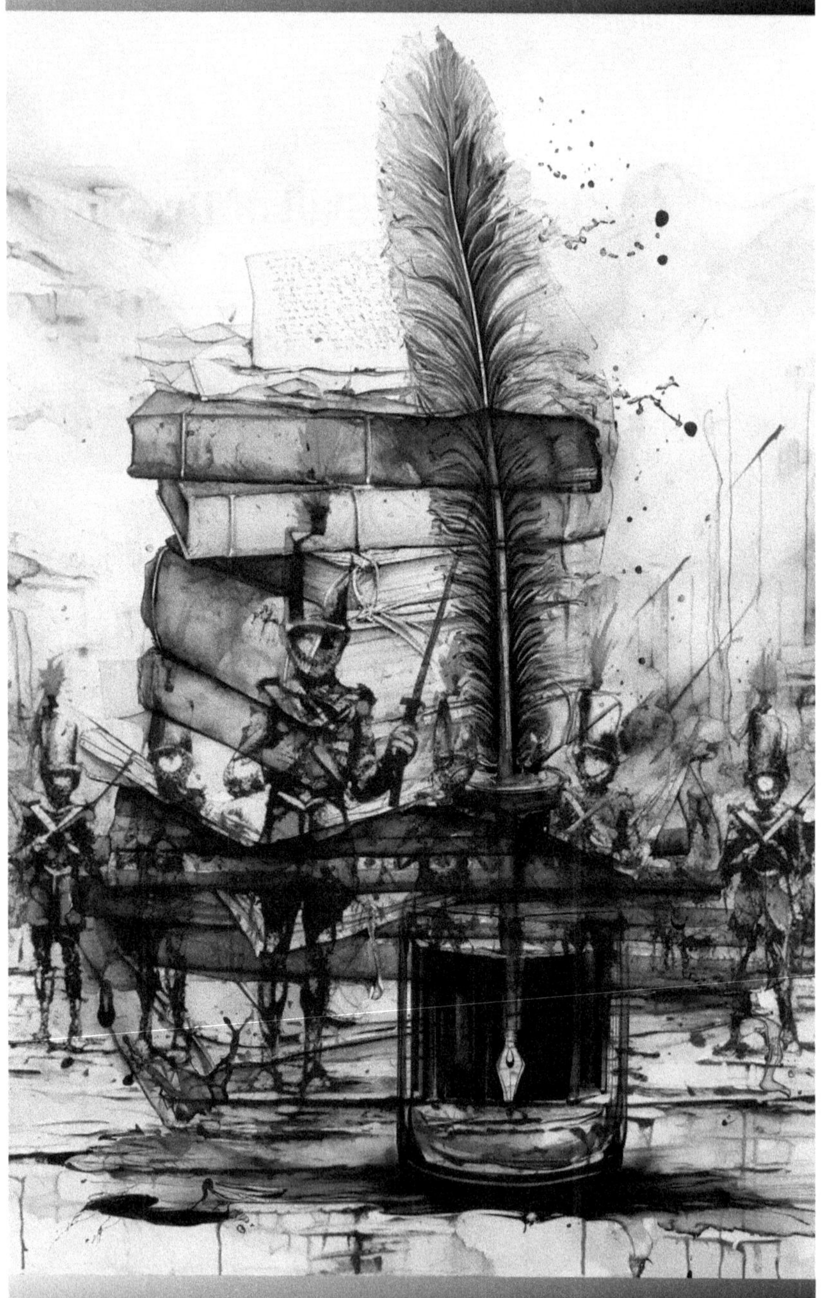

The Occupation of Drowning

I drown in refined pools
of recalcitrant, dark inkpots
alongside submerged plumage.
Liquid, ebony lines wage mute war
against one another in broad disapproval.
Martyred speech asphyxiates on
brusque parchment, bleeding
surreptitious introspection.
I drown in refined pools.

LEFT: The Song of Machination

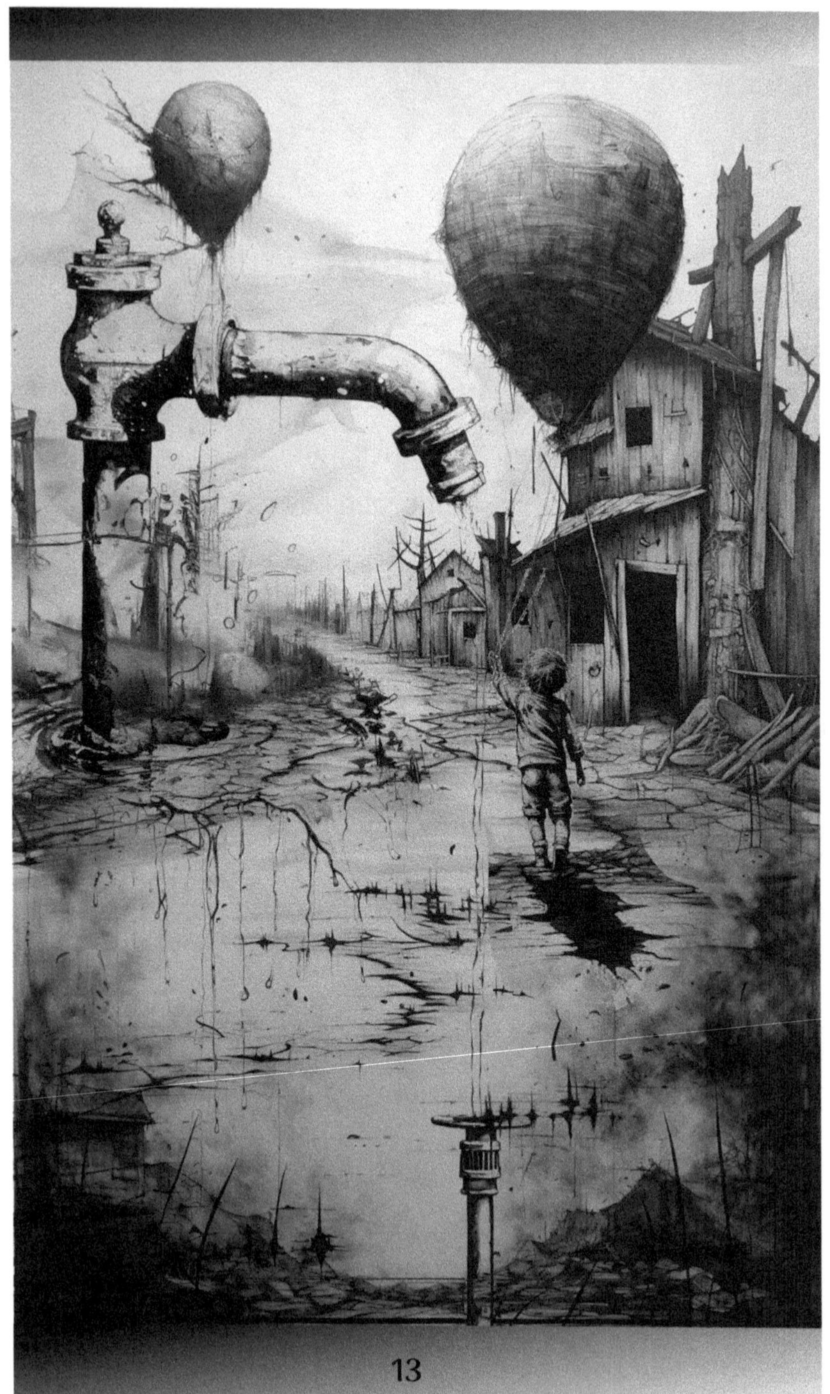

The Bias of Drowning

I drown in futile pools
of unpaid bills in a paycheck
to paycheck society with no wages.
Ballooning debt, vanishing emergency
funds and nonexistent retirement prospects.
The unearned money of lost time and
eroding confidence like the steady
drip of a leaky global economy.
I drown in futile pools.

LEFT: The Song of Obligation

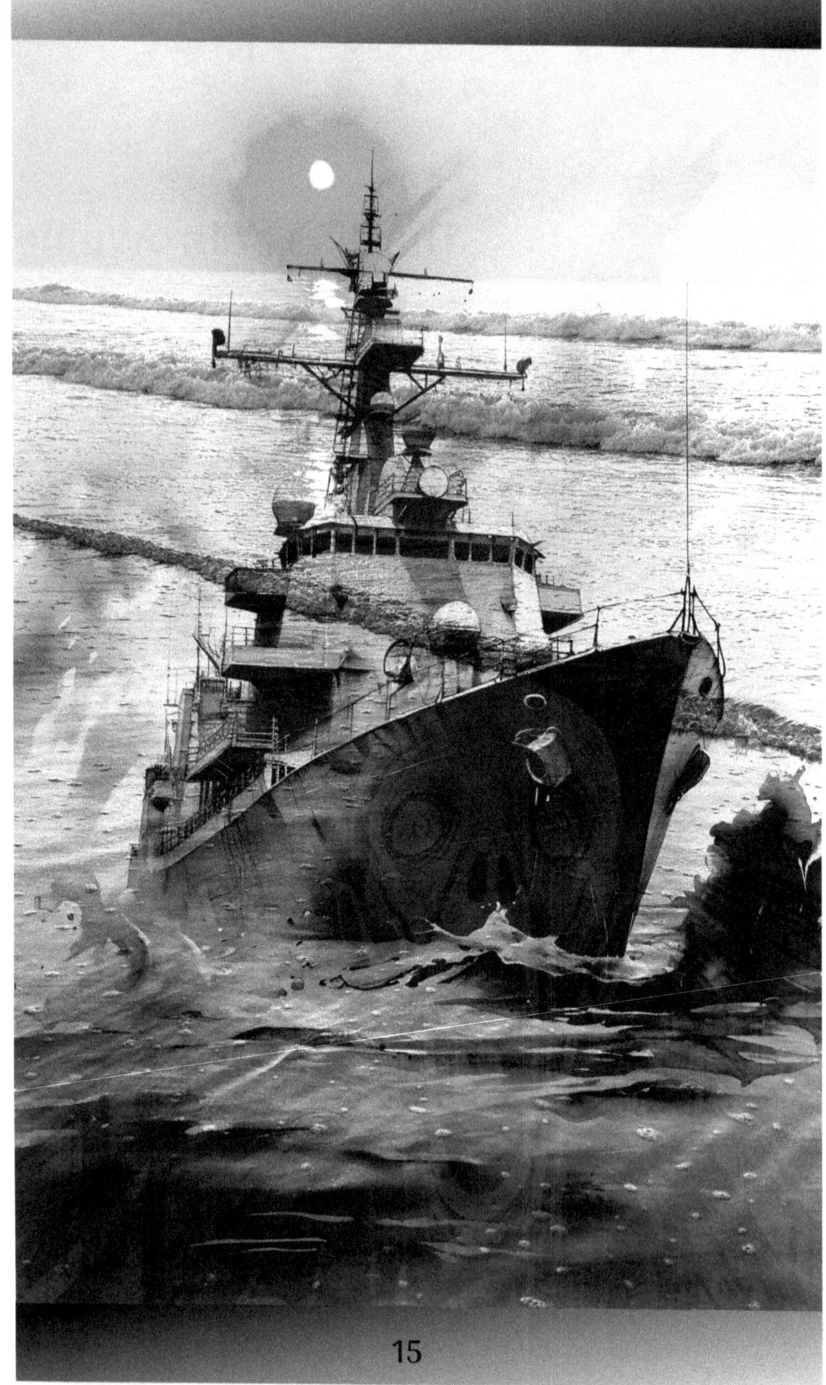

The Sterility of Drowning

I drown in scant pools
of depleted supply stocks;
fluid-filled respiratory failures.
Uncomforted by empty naval ships
swabbed decks and swabbed patients.
Cold sunsets mired in the red tape
of mistaken transfers begging
asymptomatic questioning.
I drown in scant pools.

LEFT: The Song of Enervation

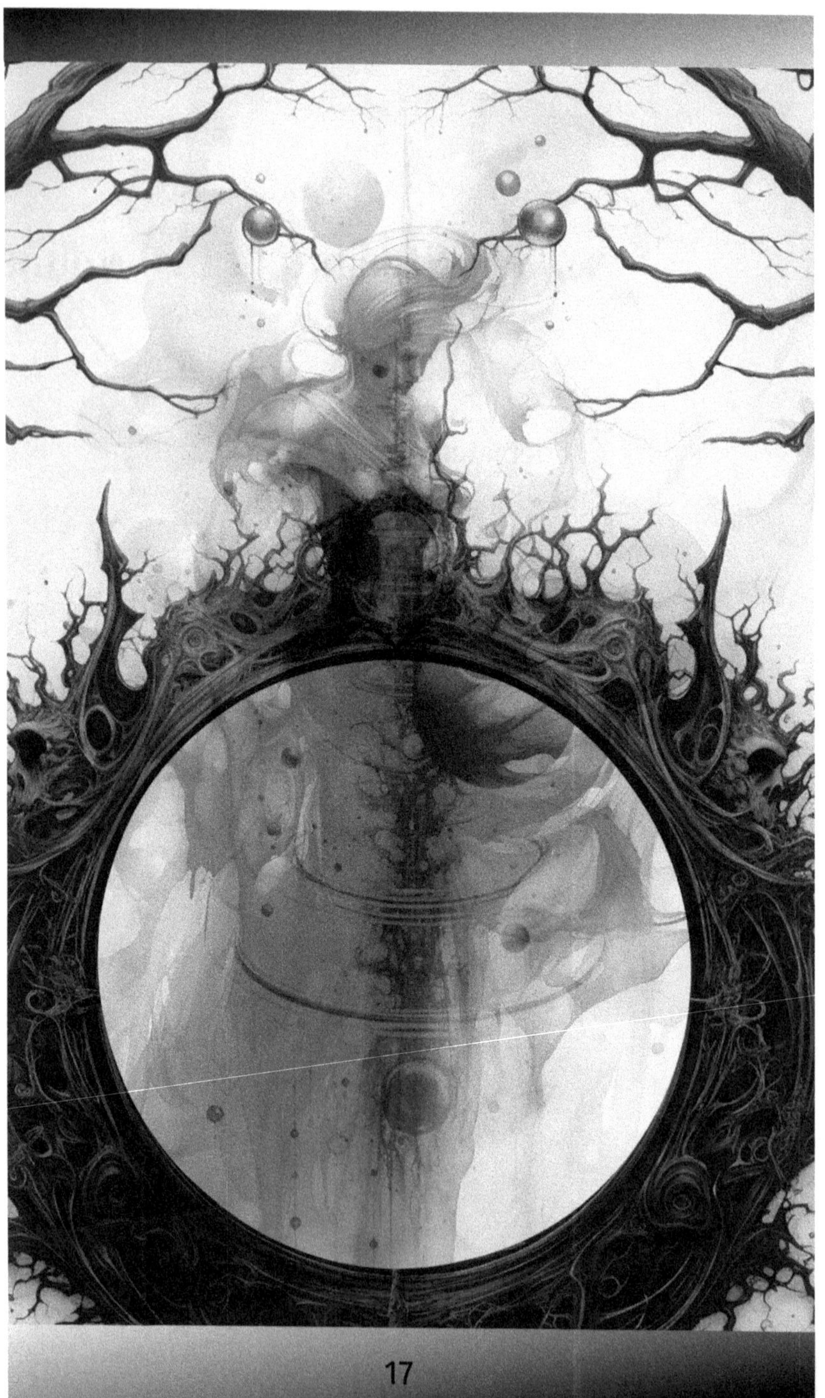

The Savagery of Drowning

I drown in feral pools
of increasing body counts
and overwhelmed sympathies.
The barbaric cacophony of frigid
cargo-holds numbing mortal reflection.
Stark death stealing corporalities,
devouring the tame nirvanas
of bewildered innocents.
I drown in feral pools.

LEFT: The Song of Apathy

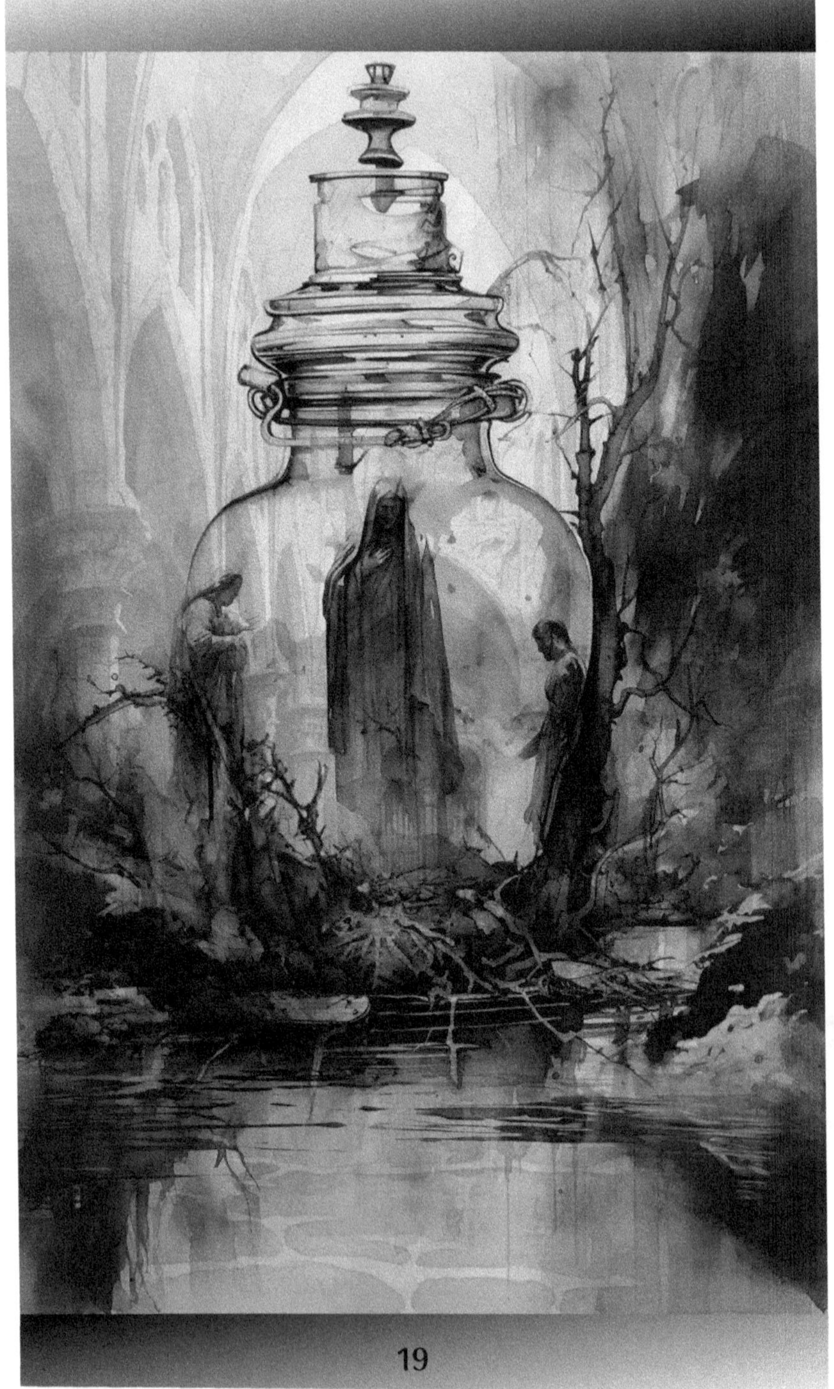

The Balm of Drowning

I drown in pious pools
of sanctified purification;
holy-drenched enlightenment.
Ritualistic waters of complication
and exclusivity disavowing proletariats.
Nihilistic mausoleums atoning
for iconoclastic baptismals
in immaculate cathedrals.
I drown in pious pools.

LEFT: The Song of Anethesia

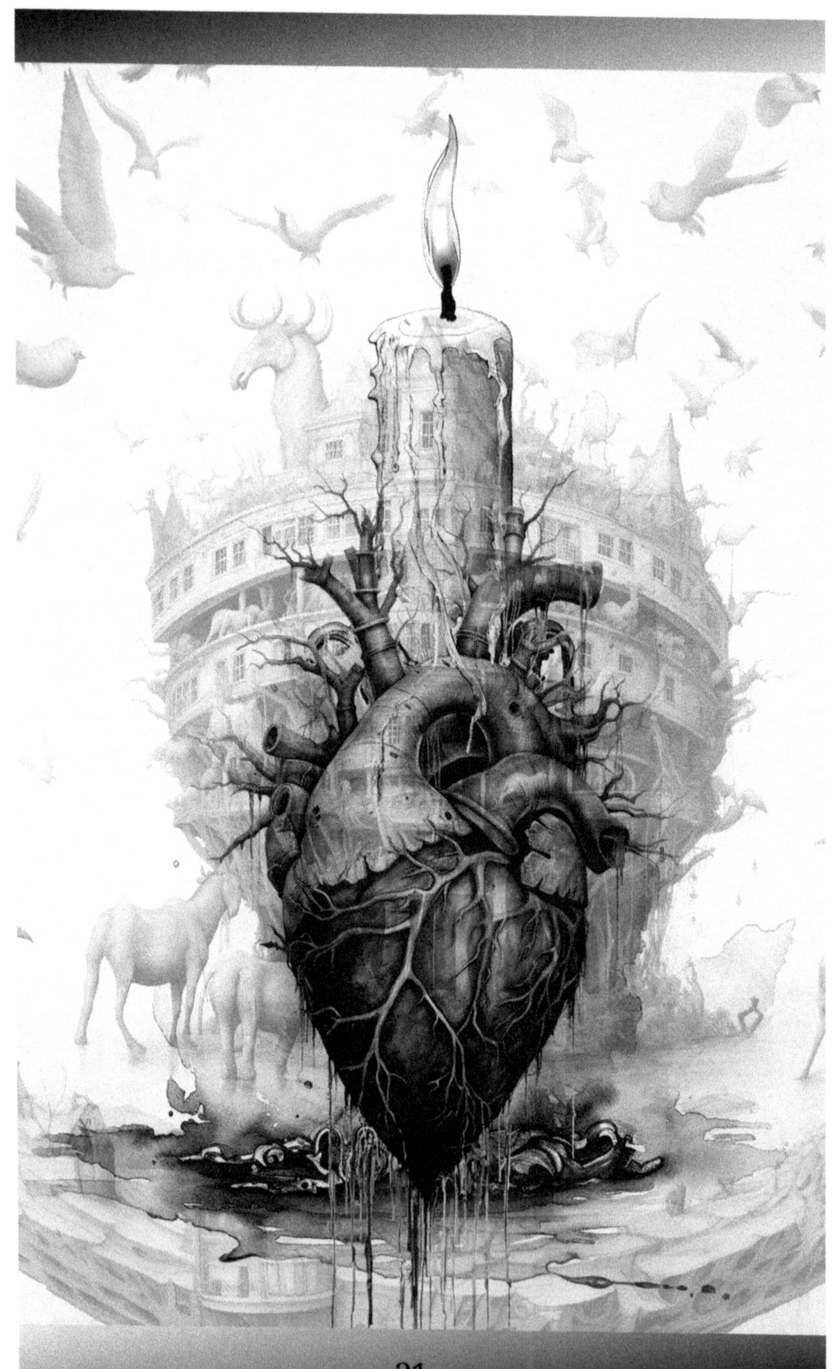

The Yarn of Drowning

I drown in idle pools
of discarded remembrance
and saturnine understandings.
The illimitable abyss of treasured
falsehoods and obfuscatory realities.
Cerebral custodian of ancestral
half-truths; fictional legacies
recounted by candlelight.
I drown in idle pools.

LEFT: The Song of Abstraction

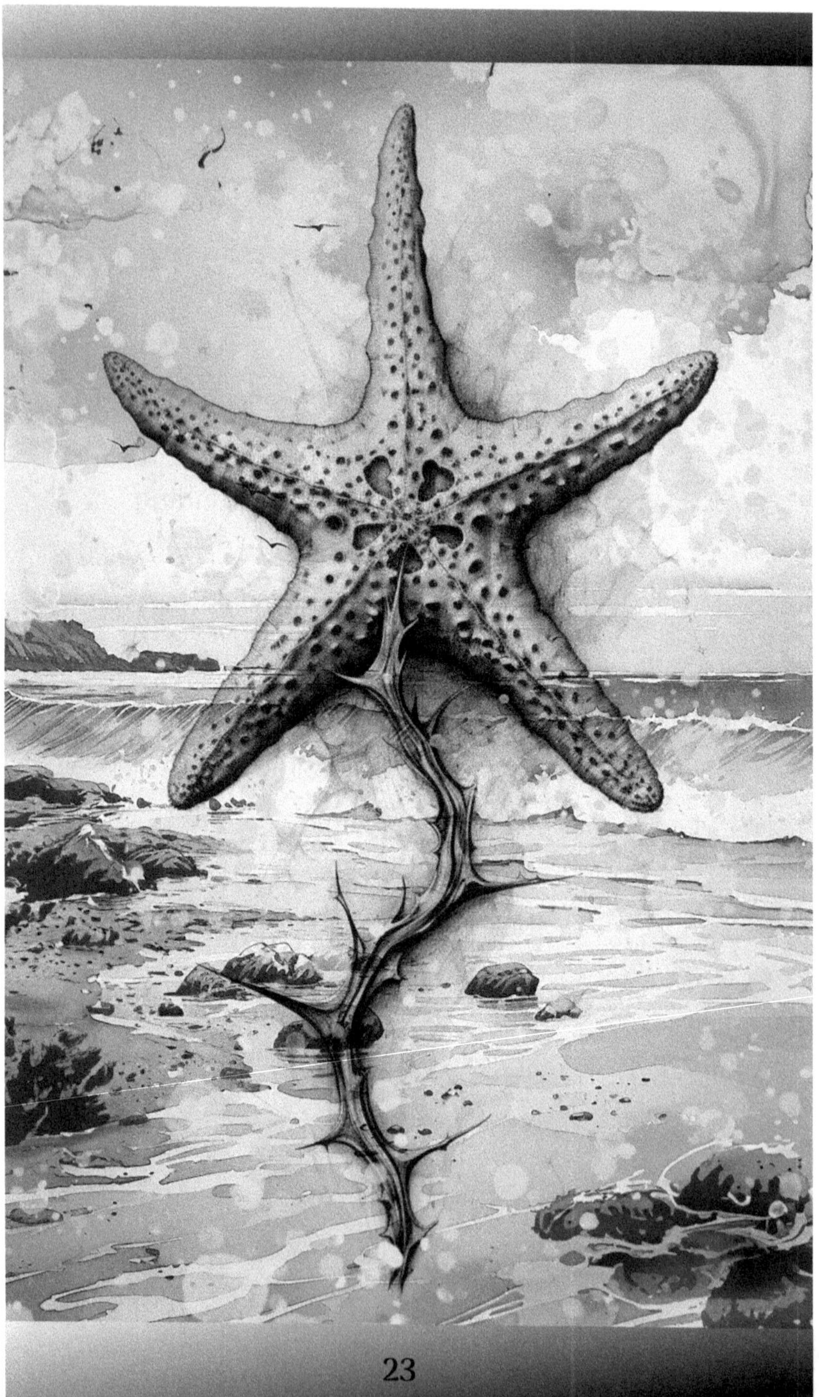

The Isolation of Drowning

I drown in shallow pools
on confined, rocky shorelines
of sequestered, teal depressions.
Currentless basins of retreated sea
evanescing in sunbaked vulnerability.
Intertidal solitude succumbing to
the inert languor of low tide's
oxygen-diminished depths.
I drown in shallow pools.

LEFT: The Song of Entrancement

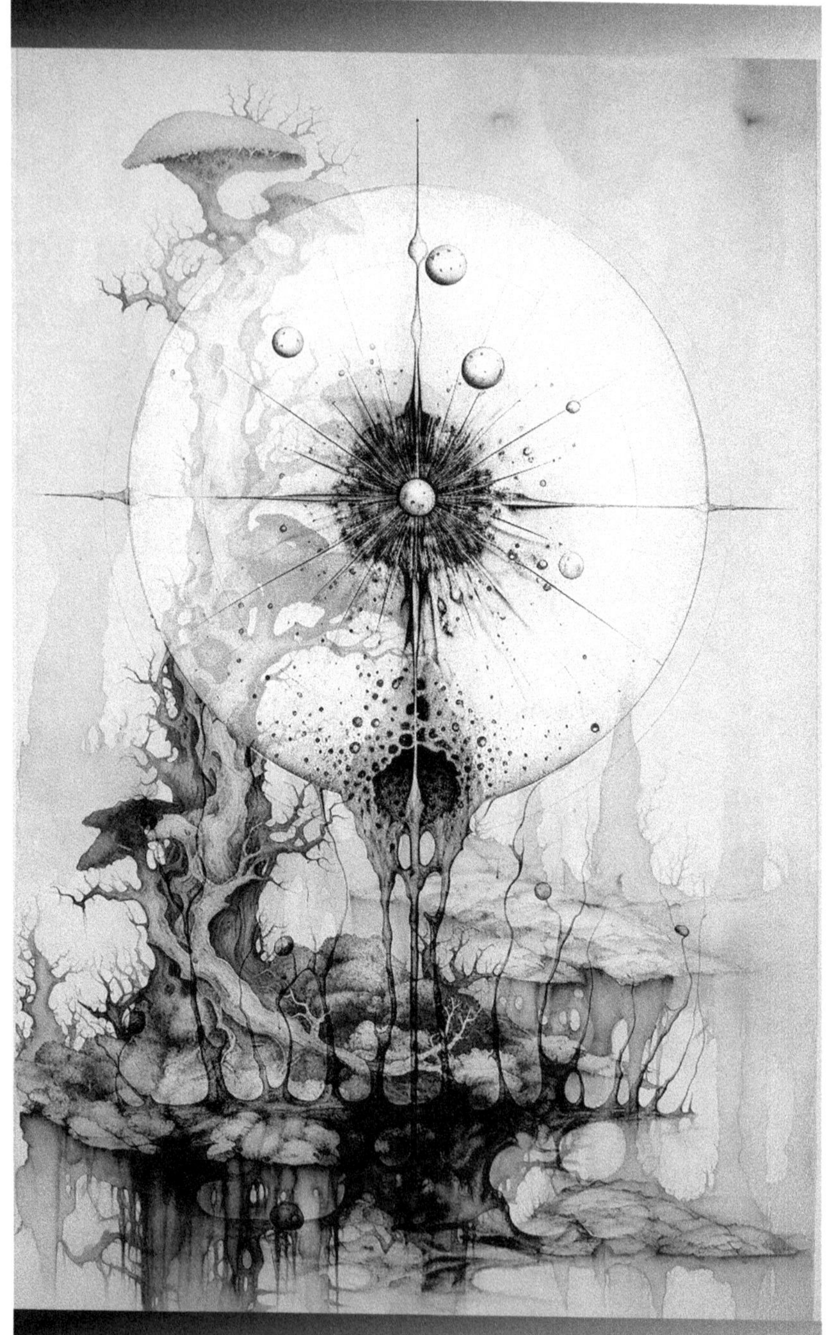

The Stench of Drowning

I drown in foul pools
of pandemic proportions
alongside isolated multitudes.
Cacophonous distortions limitless
plunge into swampy, synthetic lagoons.
Mired truth atrophied in putrefied
platitudes, and stale intentions
of overflowed negligence.
I drown in foul pools.

LEFT: The Song of Exhaustion

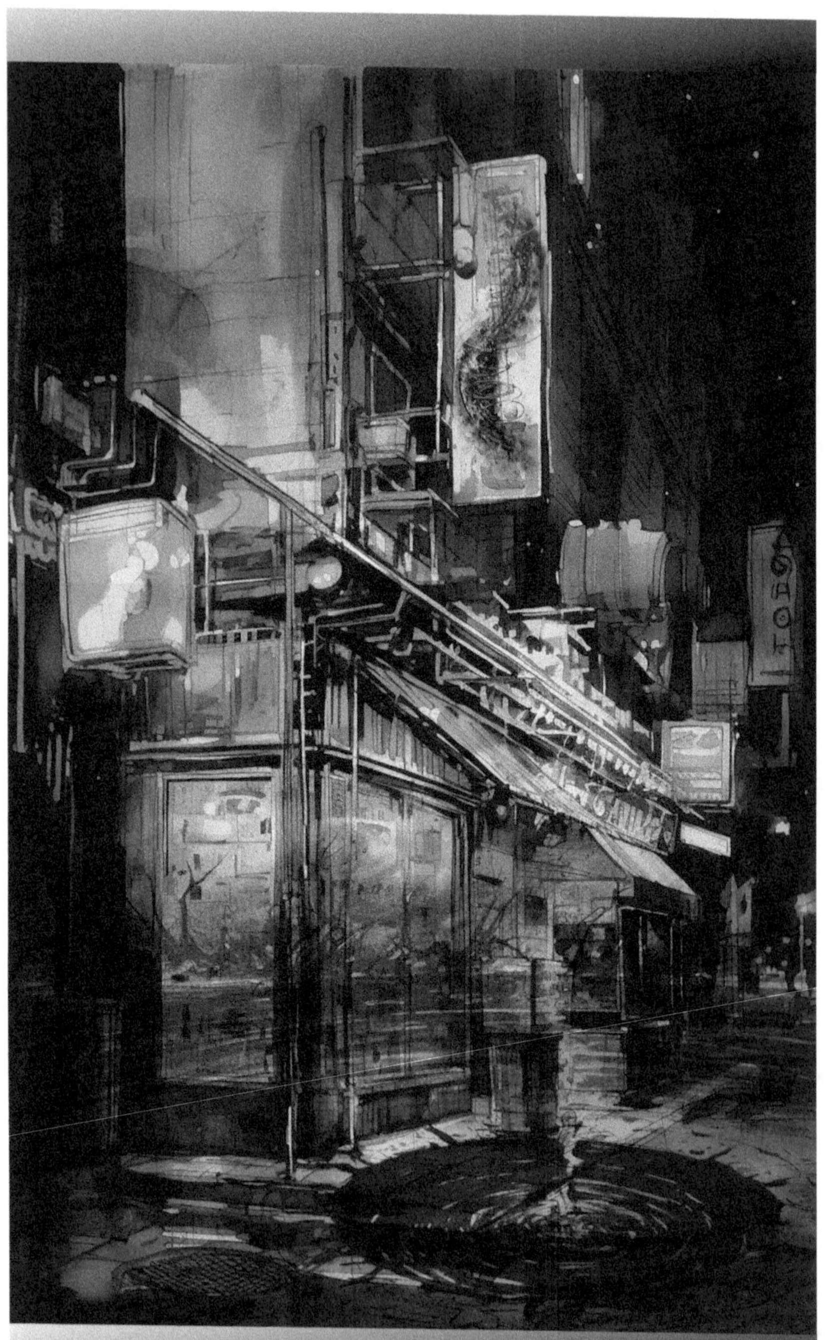

The Verity of Drowning

I drown in manic pools
of exhilarating intoxication
and frenetic, mercurial euphoria.
Reservoirs of dark agitation and feral
strength engulfing temperate comportment.
Refracted souls' aberrant stirrings mix
buoyant neuroticism and visceral
phobias under neon spotlight.
I drown in manic pools.

LEFT: The Song of Turbulence

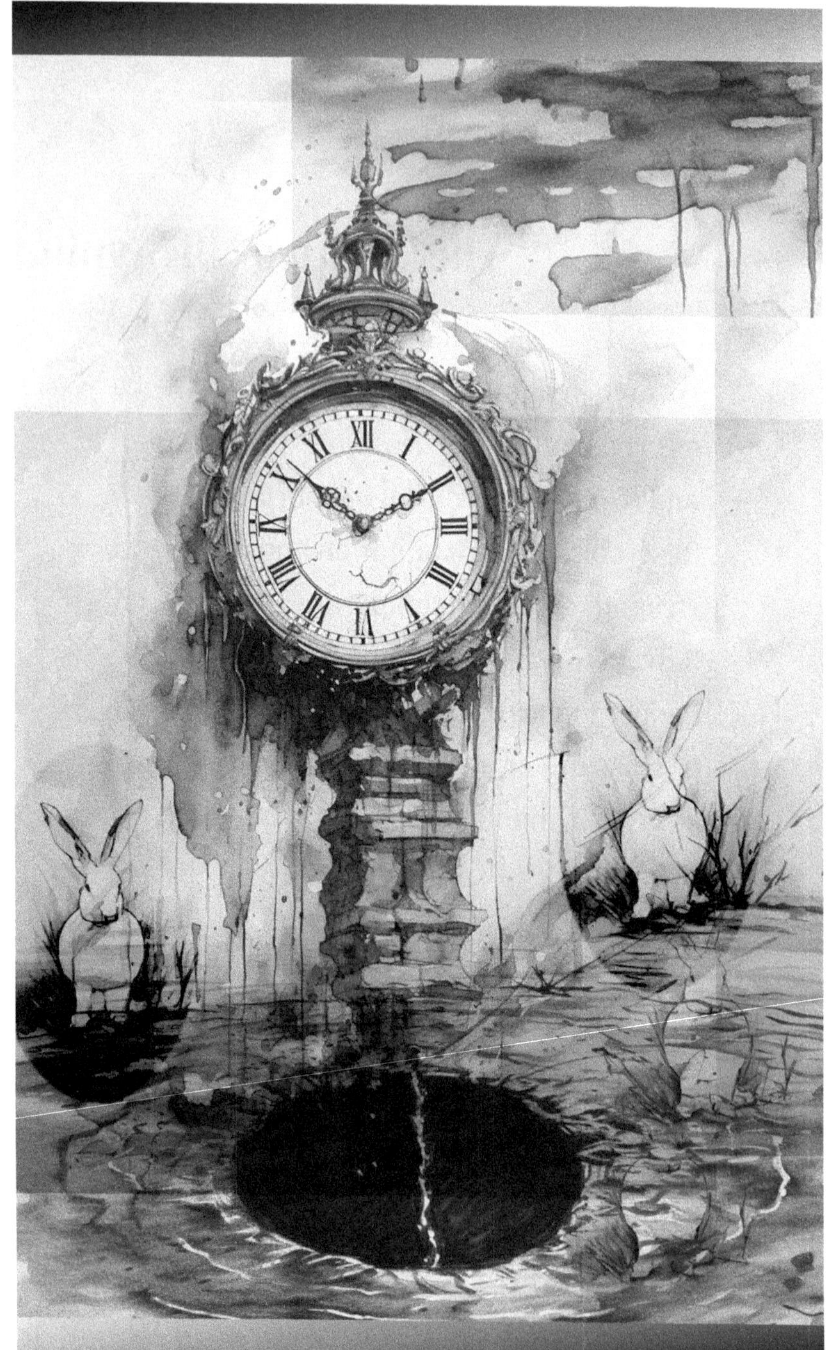

The Ease of Drowning

I drown in deep pools
of cold tears accumulated
amidst the effortless gait of time.
Absentminded flow of saline gaining
fluid-speed into waterlogged rabbit holes.
Facile vanquishing of gravitational pull,
descending in natural exhaustion,
unable to persevere upright.
I drown in deep pools.

LEFT: The Song of Paralysis

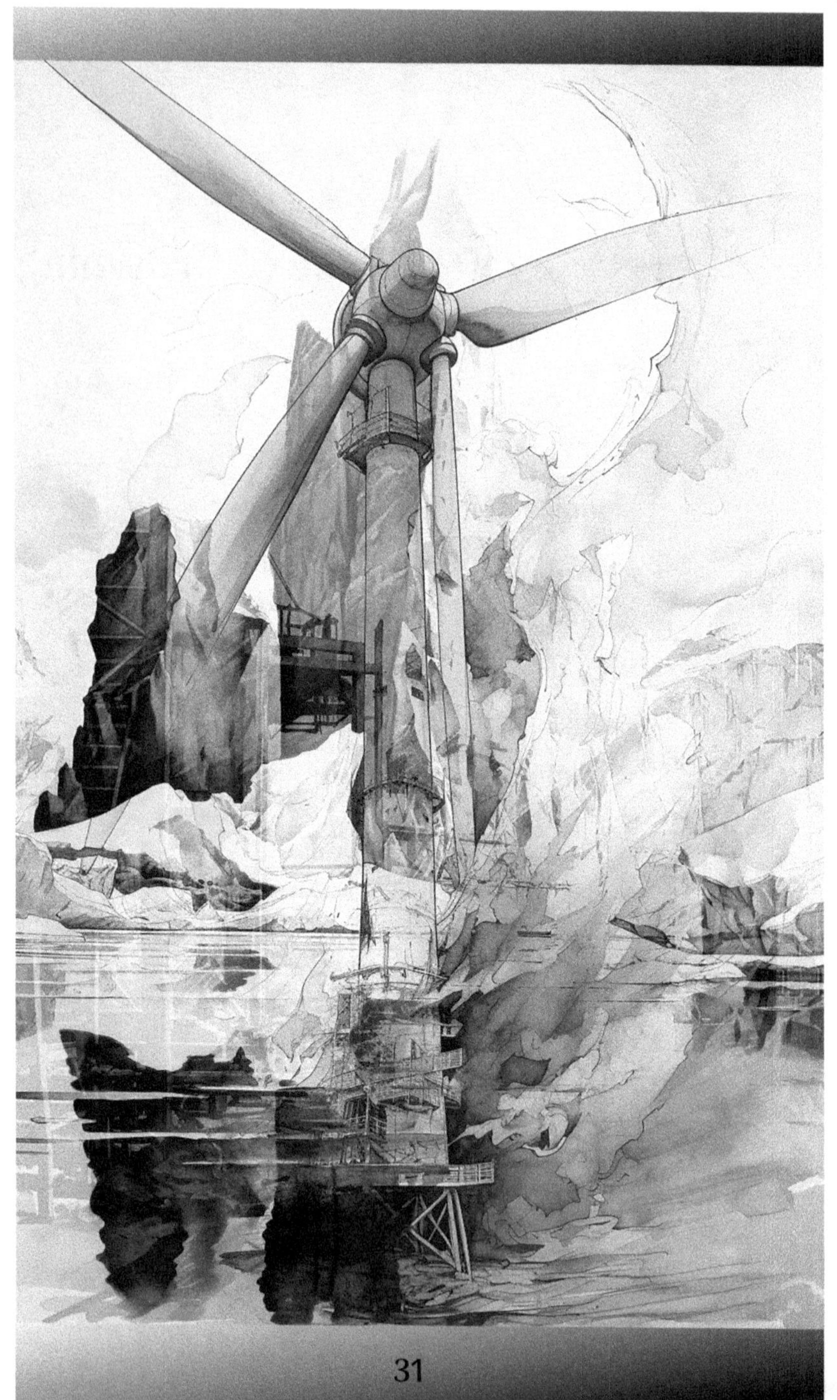

The Neutrality of Drowning

I drown in potent pools
of desecrated environment
amid the faltering of fossil fuels.
The ambivalence and slow dissolution
of warming glaciers and heated discourse.
Social norms and climate protections
gutted by cancerous windmills
across chemical waterways.
I drown in potent pools.

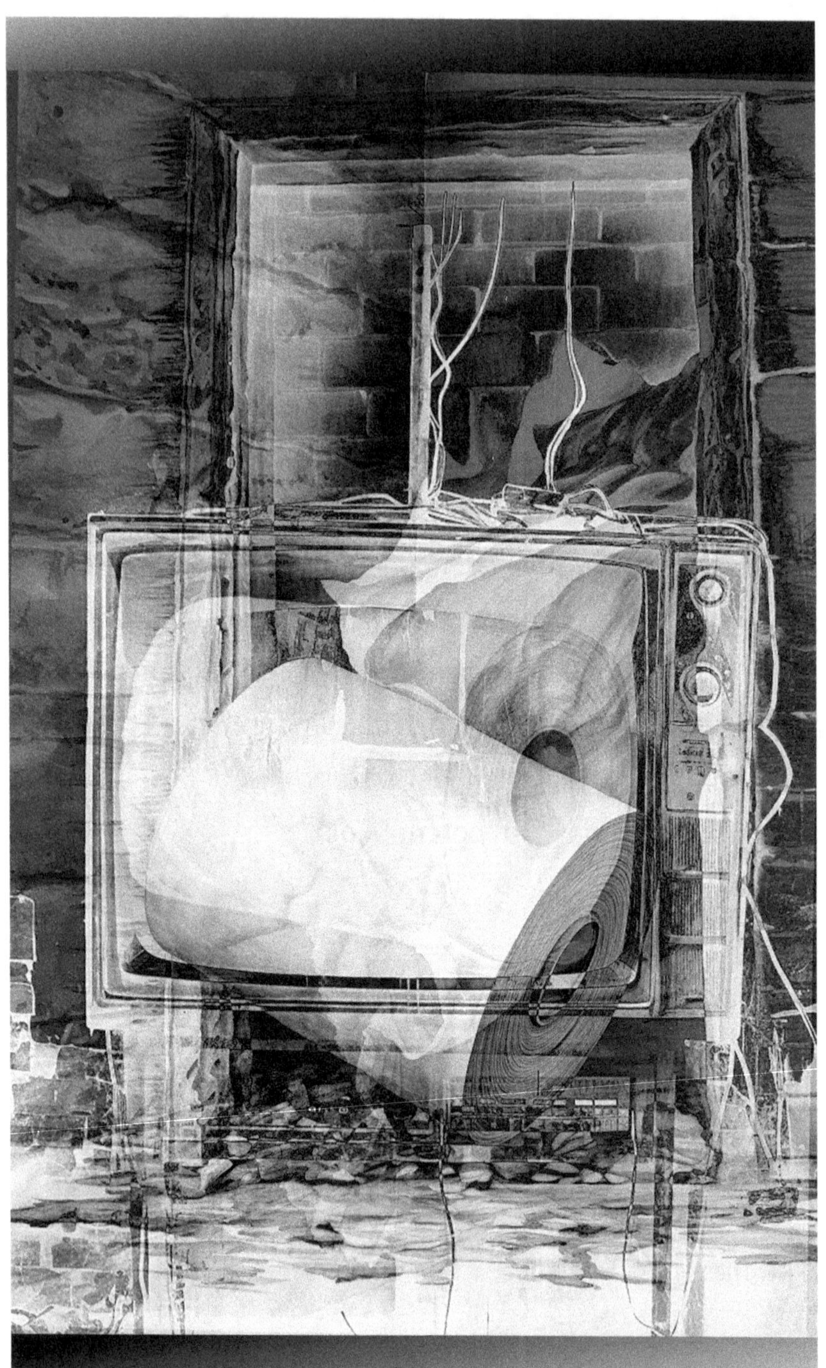

The Toxicity of Drowning

I drown in ample pools

of contradictory guidelines

from rumor mills' misinformation.

Indiscernible fact from fiction decries

widespread panic; sensational fake news.

The dangerous cures of home remedy,

spreading hysteria, self-diagnosis

and toilet paper hoarding.

I drown in ample pools.

LEFT: The Song of Fluctuation

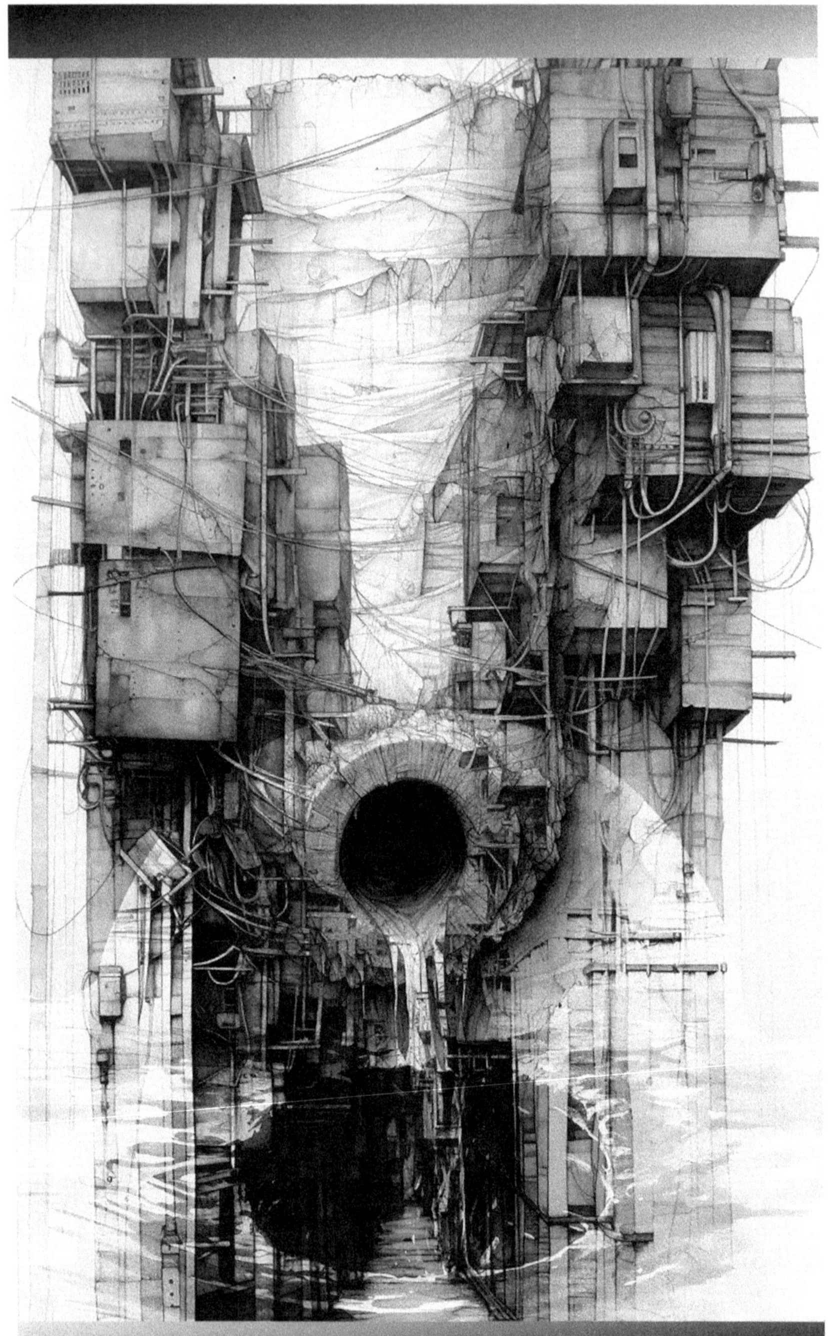

The Obeisance of Drowning

I drown in insipid pools
of copper channels ceding
life-blood to introverted labor.
Shifting conglomerate bandwidth
in fluctuating capacity and loud curses.
Crawling web and surging hexes
the substitute normal of newly
indoctrinated teleworkers.
I drown in insipid pools.

LEFT: The Song of Fealty

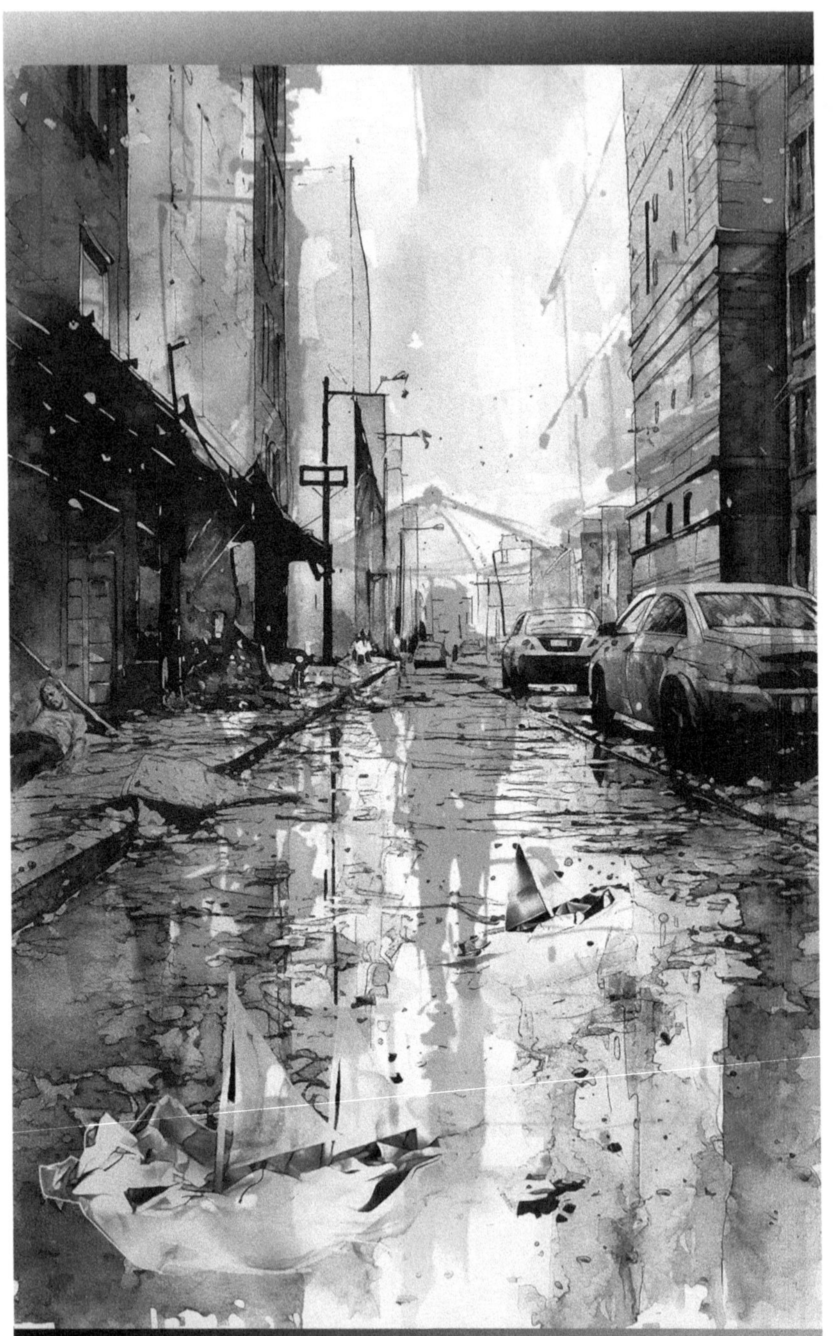

The Craft of Drowning

I drown in thick pools
of gushing acid raindrops
battering skiffs in the torrent.
Corrosive precipitation eroding
diminutive vessels down boulevards.
The crude debris of overwhelmed
gutters spewing despondent
catamarans into tempest.
I drown in thick pools.

LEFT: The Song of Transience

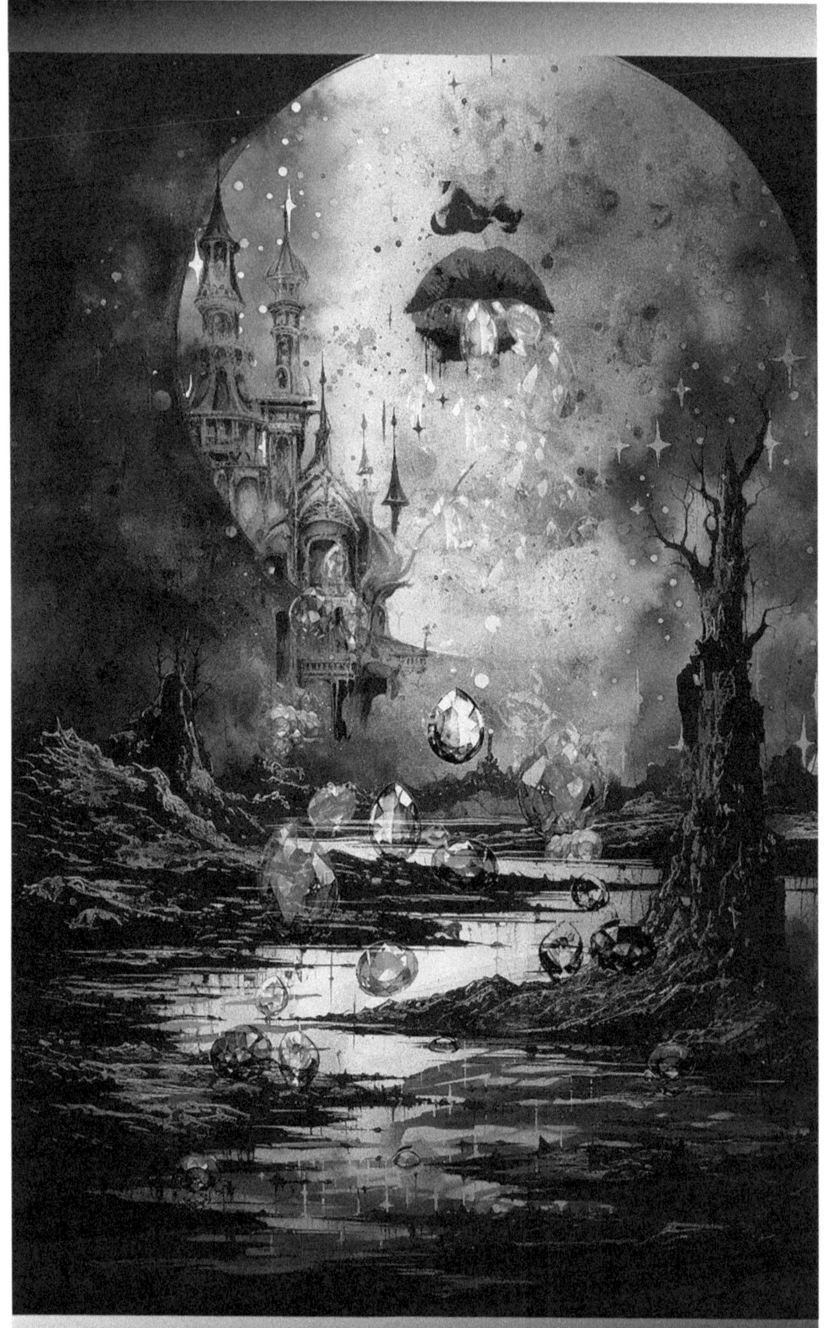

The Lesson of Drowning

I drown in vast pools
of pitch-black expanses
forewarning starlit heavens.
Celestial collapse of resplendent,
jeweled-adornment into somber death.
The breath of Zephyrus exhaled
upon effulgent Elysian field's
nonextant, benign souls.
I drown in vast pools.

LEFT: The Song of Prescience

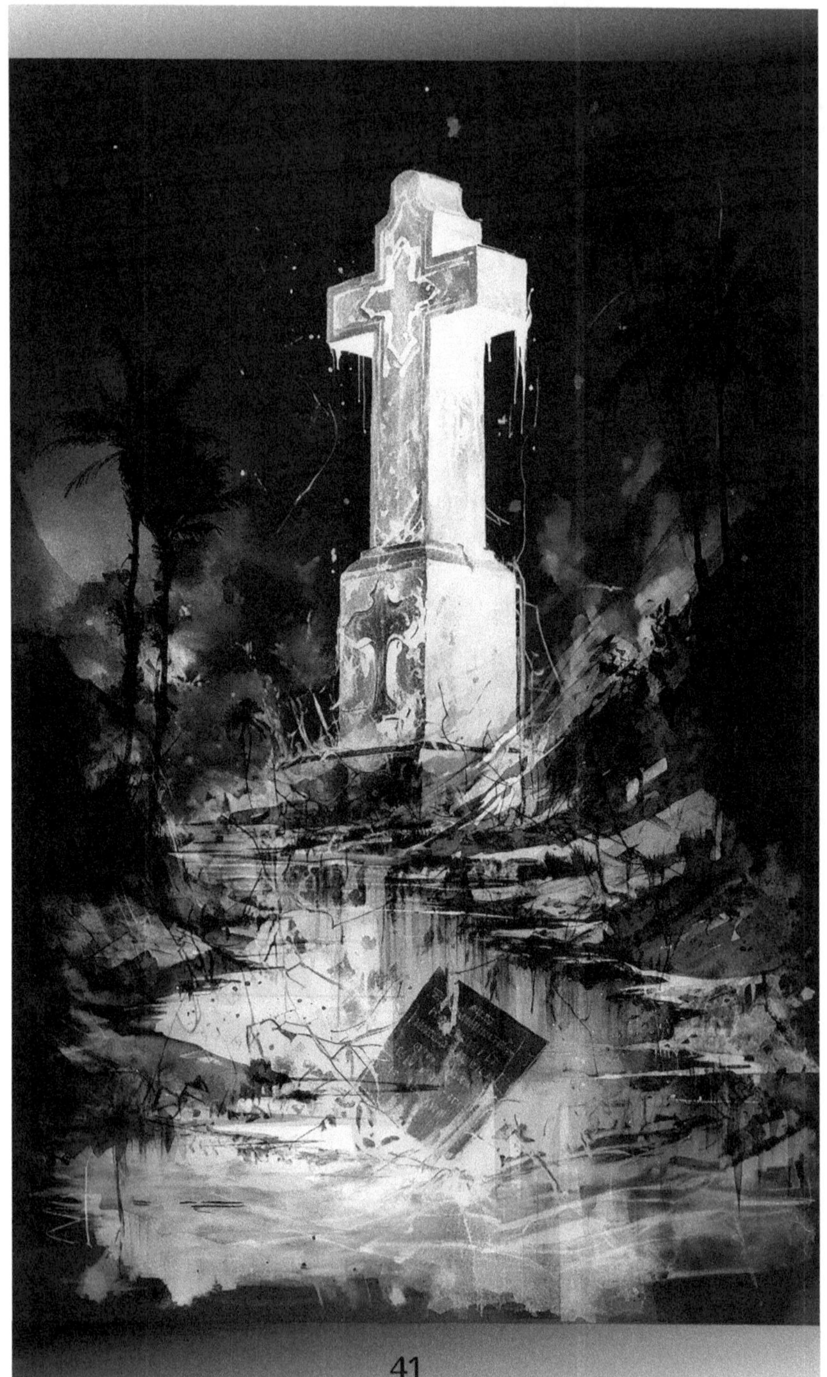

The Illusion of Drowning

I drown in abrupt pools
of coruscating false mirages
from decimated scorched-earth.
Fugacious waters of luminescence
and delusion saturating consciousness.
Contrived oasis defrauding breath
from parched lips and ravaged
lungs in transitory shrines.
I drown in abrupt pools.

LEFT: The Song of Pretense